FRANCIS

APOSTOLIC CONSTITUTION
VULTUM DEI QUAERERE
ON WOMEN'S CONTEMPLATIVE LIFE

1.   SEEKING THE FACE OF GOD has always been a part of our human history. From the beginning, men and women have been called to a dialogue of love with the Creator.[1] Indeed, mankind is distinguished by an irrepressible religious dimension that leads human hearts to feel the need – albeit not always consciously – to seek God, the Absolute. This quest unites all men and women of good will. Even many who claim to be non-believers acknowledge this heartfelt longing, present in all men and women who, drawn by a passionate desire for happiness and fulfilment, never remain fully satisfied.

Saint Augustine eloquently expressed this yearning in the *Confessions*: "You made us for yourself, and our hearts are restless until they find their rest in you".[2] This restlessness of heart is born of the profound intuition that it is God himself who takes the initiative; he seeks out men and women and mysteriously draws them to himself.

In seeking God, we quickly realize that no one is self-sufficient. Rather, we are called, in the light of faith, to move beyond self-centredness, drawn by God's Holy Face and by the "sacred ground of the other",[3] to an ever more profound experience of communion.

Through Baptism, every Christian and every consecrated person is called to undertake this pilgrimage of seeking the true God. By the working of the Holy Spirit, it becomes a *sequela pressius Christi* – a path of ever greater configuration to Christ the Lord.

---

[1] Cf. SECOND VATICAN ECUMENICAL COUNCIL, Pastoral Constitution *Gaudium et Spes*, 19.

[2] I, 1, 1: PL 32, 661.

[3] Cf. Apostolic Exhortation *Evangelii Gaudium* (24 November 2013), 169: *AAS* 105 (2013), 1091.

This path finds notable expression in religious consecration and, in a particular way, in the monastic life, which, from its origins, was seen as a specific way of living out one's baptism.

2.   Consecrated persons, by virtue of their consecration, "follow the Lord in a special way, in a prophetic way".[4] They are called to recognize the signs of God's presence in daily life and wisely to discern the questions posed to us by God and the men and women of our time. The great challenge faced by consecrated persons is to persevere in seeking God "with the eyes of faith in a world which ignores his presence",[5] and to continue to offer that world Christ's life of chastity, poverty and obedience as a credible and trustworthy sign, thus becoming "a living 'exegesis' of God's word".[6]

From the origins of the life of special consecration in the Church, men and women called by God and in love with him have devoted their lives exclusively to seeking his face, longing to find and contemplate God in the heart of the world. The presence of communities set like cities on a hill or lamps on a stand (*Mt* 5:14-15), despite their simplicity of life, visibly represent the goal towards which the entire ecclesial community journeys. For the Church "advances down the paths of time with her eyes fixed on the future restor-ation of all things in Christ,[7] thus announcing in advance the glory of heaven".[8]

3.   Peter's words, "Lord, it is good for us to be here!" (*Mt* 17: 4), have a special meaning for all consecrated persons. This is particu-

---

[4] Apostolic Letter to All Consecrated Persons for the Year of Consecrated Life (21 November 2014), II, 2: *AAS* 106 (2014), 941.

[5] JOHN PAUL II, Post-Synodal Apostolic Exhortation *Vita Consecrata* (25 March 1996), 68: *AAS* 88 (1996), 443.

[6] BENEDICT XVI, Post-Synodal Apostolic Exhortation *Verbum Domini* (30 September 2010), 83: *AAS* 102 (2010), 754.

[7] JOHN PAUL II, Post-Synodal Apostolic Exhortation *Vita Consecrata* (25 March 1996), 59: *AAS* 88 (1996), 432.

[8] Cf. *Code of Canon Law*, can. 573 § 1.

4

larly the case for contemplatives. In profound communion with every other vocation of the Christian life – all of which are "like so many rays of the one light of Christ, whose radiance brightens the countenance of the Church"[9] – contemplatives "devote a great part of their day imitating the Mother of God, who diligently pondered the words and deeds of her Son (cf. *Lk* 2:19.51), and Mary of Bethany, who sat at the Lord's feet and listened attentively to his words (cf. *Lk* 10:38)".[10] Their lives, "hidden with Christ in God" (cf. *Col* 3:3), become an image of the unconditional love of the Lord, himself the first contemplative. They are so centred on Christ that they can say with the Apostle. "For to me, to live is Christ!" (*Phil* 1:21). In this way, they express the all-encompassing character at the heart of a vocation to the contemplative life.[11]

Contemplatives, as men and women immersed in human history and drawn to the splendour of Christ, "the fairest of the sons of men" (*Ps* 45:3), are set in the heart of the Church and the world.[12] In their unending search for God, they discover the principal sign and criterion of the authenticity of their consecrated life. Saint Benedict, the father of Western monasticism, emphasized that a monk is one whose entire life is devoted to seeking God. He insisted that it be determined of one aspiring to the monastic life "*si revera Deum quaerit*", whether he truly seeks God.[13]

In a particular way, down the centuries countless consecrated women have devoted, and continue to devote "the whole of their

---

[9] *Ibid.*, 16: *AAS* 88 (1996), 389.

[10] Benedict XVI, Post-Synodal Apostolic Exhortation *Verbum Domini* (30 September 2010), 83: *AAS* 102 (2010), 754.

[11] Cf. John Paul II, Post-Synodal Apostolic Exhortation *Vita Consecrata* (25 March 1996), 18: *AAS* 88 (1996), 391-392.

[12] Cf. Second Vatican Ecumenical Council, Dogmatic Constitution *Lumen Gentium*, 44; John Paul II, Post-Synodal Apostolic Exhortation *Vita Consecrata* (25 March 1996), 3 and 29: *AAS* 88 (1996), 379, 402.

[13] *Rule* 58, 7.

lives and all their activities to the contemplation of God",[14] as a sign and prophecy of the Church, virgin, spouse and mother. Their lives are a living sign and witness of the fidelity with which God, amid the events of history, continues to sustain his people.

4.   The monastic life, as an element of unity with the other Christian confessions,[15] takes on a specific form that is prophecy and sign, one that "can and ought to attract all the members of the Church to an effective and prompt fulfilment of the duties of their Christian vocation".[16] Communities of prayer, especially contemplative communities, which "by virtue of their separation from the world are all the more closely united to Christ, the heart of the world",[17] do not propose a more perfect fulfilment of the Gospel. Rather, by living out the demands of Baptism, they constitute an instance of discernment and a summons to the service of the whole Church. Indeed, they are a signpost pointing to a journey and quest, a reminder to the entire People of God of the primary and ultimate meaning of the Christian life.[18]

ESTEEM, PRAISE AND THANKSGIVING FOR CONSECRATED LIFE
AND CLOISTERED CONTEMPLATIVE LIFE

5.   From the earliest centuries the Church has shown great esteem and sincere love for those men and women who, in docility to the Father's call and the promptings of the Spirit, have chosen to follow

---

[14] JOHN PAUL II, Post-Synodal Apostolic Exhortation *Vita Consecrata* (25 March 1996), 8: *AAS* 88 (1996), 382-383.

[15] ID., Apostolic Letter *Orientale Lumen* (2 May 1995), 9: *AAS* 87 (1995), 754.

[16] SECOND VATICAN ECUMENICAL COUNCIL, Dogmatic Constitution *Lumen Gentium*, 44, 1.

[17] BENEDICT XVI, Post-Synodal Apostolic Exhortation *Verbum Domini* (30 September 2010), 83: *AAS* 102 (2010), 754.

[18] Cf. SECOND VATICAN ECUMENICAL COUNCIL, Decree *Perfectae Caritatis*, 5.

Christ "more closely",[19] dedicating themselves to him with an undivided heart (cf. *1 Cor* 7:34). Moved by unconditional love for Christ and all humanity, particularly the poor and the suffering, they are called to reproduce in a variety of forms – as consecrated virgins, widows, hermits, monks and religious – the earthly life of Jesus in chastity, poverty and obedience.[20]

The contemplative monastic life, made up mainly of women, is rooted in the silence of the cloister; it produces a rich harvest of grace and mercy. Women's contemplative life has always represented in the Church, and for the Church, her praying heart, a storehouse of grace and apostolic fruitfulness, and a visible witness to the mystery and rich variety of holiness.[21]

Originating in the individual experience of virgins consecrated to Christ, the natural fruit of a need to respond with love to the love of Christ the Bridegroom, this life soon took form as a definite state and an order recognized by the Church, which began to receive public professions of virginity. With the passage of time, most consecrated virgins united in forms of common life that the Church was concerned to protect and preserve with a suitable discipline. The cloister was meant to preserve the spirit and the strictly contemplative aim of these houses. The gradual interplay between the working of the Spirit, present in the heart of believers and inspiring new forms of discipleship, and the maternal solicitude of the Church, gave rise to the forms of contemplative and wholly contemplative life that we know today.[22] In the West, the contemplative spirit found expression in a multiplicity of charisms, whereas in the

---

[19] *Ibid.*, 1.

[20] Cf. JOHN PAUL II, Post-Synodal Apostolic Exhortation *Vita Consecrata* (25 March 1996), 14: *AAS* 88 (1996), 387.

[21] Cf. SECOND VATICAN ECUMENICAL COUNCIL, Dogmatic Constitution *Lumen Gentium*, 46; Decree *Christus Dominus*, 35; Decree *Perfectae Caritatis*, 7 and 9; *Code of Canon Law*, can. 674.

[22] Cf. *Code of Canon Law,* can. 667 § 2-3.

East it maintained great unity,[23] but always as a testimony to the richness and beauty of a life devoted completely to God.

Over the centuries, the experience of these sisters, centred on the Lord as their first and only love (cf. *Hos* 2:21-25), has brought forth abundant fruits of holiness and mission. How much has the apostolate been enriched by the prayers and sacrifices radiating from monasteries! And how great is the joy and prophecy proclaimed to the world by the silence of the cloister!

For the fruits of holiness and grace that the Lord has always bestowed through women's monastic life, let us sing to "the Most High, the Almighty and good Lord" the hymn of thanksgiving *"Laudato si'*!"[24]

6.   Dear contemplative sisters, without you what would the Church be like, or without all those others living on the fringes of humanity and ministering in the outposts of evangelization? The Church greatly esteems your life of complete self-giving. The Church counts on your prayers and on your self-sacrifice to bring today's men and women to the good news of the Gospel. The Church needs you!

It is not easy for the world, or at least that large part of it dominated by the mindset of power, wealth and consumerism, to understand your particular vocation and your hidden mission; and yet it needs them immensely. The world needs you every bit as much as a sailor on the high seas needs a beacon to guide him to a safe haven. Be beacons to those near to you and, above all, to those far away. Be torches to guide men and women along their journey through the dark night of time. Be sentinels of the morning (cf. *Is* 21:11-12), heralding the dawn (cf. *Lk* 1:78). By your transfigured life, and with simple words pondered in silence, shows us the One who is the way, and the truth and the life (cf. *Jn* 14:6), the Lord who alone brings us

[23] Cf. JOHN PAUL II, Apostolic Letter *Orientale Lumen* (2 May 1995), 9: *AAS* 87 (1995), 754.

[24] FRANCIS OF ASSISI, *Canticle of the Creatures*, 1: FF 263.

8

fulfilment and bestows life in abundance (cf. *Jn* 10:10). Cry out to us, as Andrew did to Simon: "We have found the Lord" (cf. *Jn* 1:40). Like Mary Magdalene on Easter morning, announce to us: "I have seen the Lord!" (*Jn* 20:18). Cherish the prophetic value of your lives of self-sacrifice. Do not be afraid to live fully the joy of evangelical life, in accordance with your charism.

THE CHURCH'S ACCOMPANIMENT AND GUIDANCE

7. The magisterium of the Councils and the Popes has always shown a particular concern for all forms of consecrated life through the promulgation of important documents. Among these, special attention needs to be given to two great documents of the Second Vatican Council: the Dogmatic Constitution on the Church *Lumen Gentium* and the Decree on the Renewal of Religious Life *Perfectae Caritatis*.

The first of these sets the consecrated life within the ecclesiology of the People of God by virtue of the common call to holiness rooted in the consecration of Baptism.[25] The second summons all consecrated persons to a fitting renewal in accordance with the changed conditions of the times. To guide such a renewal, the document proposes the following indispensable criteria: fidelity to Christ, to the Gospel, to one's own charism, to the Church, and to the men and women of our time.[26]

Nor can we pass over the Post-Synodal Apostolic Exhortation *Vita Consecrata* of my predecessor, Saint John Paul II. This document, which reaped the rich harvest of the Synod of Bishops on Consecrated Life, contains elements that remain important for the continued renewal of consecrated life and its clear witness to the Gospel in our day (cf. especially Nos. 59 and 68).

[25] SECOND VATICAN ECUMENICAL COUNCIL, Dogmatic Constitution *Lumen Gentium*, 44.

[26] Cf. Decree *Perfectae Caritatis*, 2.

We can also add the following documents as evidence of the constant and helpful guidance provided to the contemplative life:

– The Directives of the Congregation for the Institutes of Consecrated Life and Societies of Apostolic Life (CICLSAL) *Potissimum Institutioni* (2 February 1990), dealt extensively with the specifically contemplative form of consecrated life (Chapter IV, 78-85).

– The Inter-Dicasterial Document *Sviluppi* (6 January 1992) dealt with the issue of diminishing vocations to the consecrated life in general and, to a lesser extent, the contemplative life (No. 81).

– The *Catechism of the Catholic Church*, promulgated by the Apostolic Constitution *Fidei Depositum* (11 October 1992), is very helpful for enabling the faithful to understand your form of life; this is particularly the case with Nos. 915-933, which treats all its forms. No. 1672 deals with your non-sacramental consecration and with the blessing of Abbots and Abbesses. Nos. 1974 and 2102 link the Ten Commandments to the profession of the evangelical counsels. No. 2518 presents the close bond between the purity of heart spoken of in the Beatitudes as promising the vision of God, and love of the truths of the faith. Nos. 1691 and 2687 praise the persevering intercession made to God by contemplative monasteries – unique places where personal prayer and prayer in community are harmoniously joined, while No. 2715 notes that the prerogative of contemplatives is to keep their gaze fixed on Jesus and the mysteries of his life and ministry.

– The CICLSAL Instruction *Congregavit Nos* (2 February 1994) at Nos. 10 and 34 linked silence and solitude with the profound demands of a community of fraternal life, and stressed that separation from the world is consistent with a daily atmosphere of prayer.

– The CICLSAL Instruction *Verbi Sponsa, Ecclesia* (13 May 1999) in Articles 1-8 offered an impressive historical-systematic synthesis of previous teachings of the magisterium on the eschatological and missionary significance of the cloistered life of contemplative nuns.

– Finally, the CICLSAL Instruction *Starting Afresh from Christ* (19 May 2002) urged all consecrated persons to contemplate unceasingly the face of Christ. It presents cloistered monks and nuns as the summit of the Church's choral praise and silent prayer (No. 25), and at the same time praises them for having always kept the Liturgy of the Hours and the Eucharistic celebration at the centre of their daily life (ibid.)

8. Fifty years after the Second Vatican Council, after due consultation and careful discernment, I have considered it necessary to offer the Church, with special reference to monasteries of the Latin rite, the present Apostolic Constitution. It takes into account both the intense and fruitful journey taken by the Church in recent decades in the light of the teachings of the Second Vatican Ecumenical Council and a changed social and cultural situation. In these past decades, we have seen rapid historical changes that call for dialogue. At the same time, the foundational values of contemplative life need to be maintained. Through these values – silence, attentive listening, the call to an interior life, stability – contemplative life can and must challenge the contemporary mindset.

With this document I wish to reaffirm my personal esteem, together with the gratitude of the entire Church, for the unique form of *sequela Christi* practised by nuns of contemplative life; for many, it is an entirely contemplative life, a priceless and indispensable gift which the Holy Spirit continues to raise up in the Church.

Wherever necessary or fitting, the Congregation for Institutes of Consecrated Life and Societies of Apostolic Life will deal with particular questions and reach agreements with the Congregation for the Evangelization of Peoples and the Congregation for the Oriental Churches.

9.   From the first centuries, contemplative life has always been present in the Church, alternating periods of great vigour and others of decline. This has been due to the constant presence of the Lord, together with the Church's own capacity to renew and adapt herself to changes in society. The contemplative life has always continued to seek the face of God and to preserve unconditional love for Christ as its hallmark.

The consecrated life is a history of passionate love for the Lord and for humanity. In the contemplative life, this history unfolds day after day in a passionate quest to see the face of God in intimate relationship with him. As contemplative women, you respond to Christ the Lord, "who first loved us" (*1 Jn* 4:19) and "gave himself up for us" (*Eph* 5:2), by offering your entire life, living in him and for him, "for the praise of his glory" (*Eph* 1:12). Through this life of contemplation, you are the voice of the Church as she ceaselessly praises, thanks, implores and intercedes for all mankind. Through your prayer, you are co-workers of God, helping the fallen members of his glorious body to rise again.[27]

In your personal and communitarian prayer, you discover the Lord as the treasure of your life (cf. *Lk* 12:34), your good, "utter goodness, the supreme good", your "wealth and sufficiency".[28] You come to see, with steadfast faith, that "God alone suffices",[29] and that you have chosen the better part (cf. *Lk* 10:42). You have surrendered your life and fixed your gaze upon the Lord, retreating into the cell of your heart (cf. *Mt* 6:5) in the inhabited solitude of the cloister and fraternal life in community. In this way, you have become an image of Christ who seeks to encounter the Father on the heights (cf. *Mt* 14:23).

---

[27] Cf. CLARE OF ASSISI, *Third Letter to Agnes of Bohemia*, 8: FF 2886.

[28] FRANCIS OF ASSISI, *Lodi al Dio Altissimo*, 3.5: FF 261.

[29] TERESA OF AVILA, *Obras completas. Poesías*, Editorial Monte Carmelo, Burgos, 2011, 1368.

10.   Over the centuries, the Church has always looked to Mary as the *summa contemplatrix*.[30] From the annunciation to the resurrection, through the pilgrimage of faith that reached its climax at the foot of the cross, Mary persevered in contemplation of the mystery dwelling within her. In Mary, we glimpse the mystical journey of the consecrated person, grounded in a humble wisdom that savours the mystery of the ultimate fulfilment.

Following Mary's example, the contemplative is a person centred in God and for whom God is the *unum necessarium* (cf. *Lk* 10:42), in comparison with which all else is seen from a different perspective, because seen through new eyes. Contemplatives appreciate the value of material things, yet these do not steal their heart or cloud their mind; on the contrary, they serve as a ladder to ascend to God. For the contemplative, everything "speaks"[31] of the Most High! Those who immerse themselves in the mystery of contemplation see things with spiritual eyes. This enables them to see the world and other persons as God does, whereas others "have eyes but do not see" (*Ps* 115:5; 135:16; cf. *Jer* 5:21), for they see with carnal eyes.

11.   Contemplation thus involves having, in Christ Jesus whose face is constantly turned to the Father (cf. *Jn* 1:18), a gaze transfigured by the working of the Holy Spirit, a gaze full of awe at God and his wonders. Contemplation involves having a pure mind, in which the echoes of the Word and the voice of the Spirit are felt as a soft wind (cf. *1 Kg* 19:12). It is not by chance that contemplation is born of faith; indeed, faith is both the door and the fruit of contemplation. It is only by saying with utter trust, "Here I am!" (cf. *Lk* 2:38), that one can enter into the mystery.

[30] Cf. Denis the Carthusian, *Enarrationes in cap. 3 Can. Cant.* XI, 6, in *Doctoris Ecstatici D. Dionysii Cartusiani Opera Omnia*, VII, Typis Cartusiae, Monstrolii, 1898, 361.

[31] Francis of Assisi, *Canticle of the Creatures*, 4: FF 263.

This silent and recollected peace of mind and heart can meet with subtle temptations. Your contemplation can become a spiritual combat to be fought courageously in the name of, and for the good of, the entire Church, which looks to you as faithful sentinels, strong and unyielding in battle. Among the most perilous temptations faced by contemplatives is that which the Desert Fathers called "the midday devil"; it is the temptation to listlessness, mere routine, lack of enthusiasm and paralyzing lethargy. As I noted in the Apostolic Exhortation *Evangelii Gaudium*, little by little this leads to "a tomb psychology... [that] develops and slowly transforms Christians into mummies in a museum. Disillusioned with reality, with the Church and with themselves, they experience a constant temptation to cling to a faint melancholy, lacking in hope, which seizes the heart like 'the most precious of the devil's potions'."[32]

MATTERS CALLING FOR DISCERNMENT AND RENEWED NORMS

12.   As a means of assisting contemplative women to attain the goal of their specific vocation as described above, I would invite reflection and discernment on twelve aspects of consecrated life in general and the monastic tradition in particular. These are formation, prayer, the word of God, the sacraments of the Eucharist and Reconciliation, fraternal life in community, autonomy, federations, the cloister, work, silence, the communications media and asceticism. The results of this reflection and discernment will have to be implemented in ways respectful of the specific charismatic traditions of the various monastic families. At the same time, they must respect the regulations found at the end of the present Constitution, as well as the practical guidelines soon to be issued by the Congregation for Institutes of Consecrated Life and Societies of Apostolic Life.

[32] No. 83: *AAS* 105 (2013), 1054-1055.

14

Formation

13.   The formation of consecrated persons is a process aimed at configuration to the Lord Jesus and the assimilation of his mind and heart in the complete gift of self to the Father. This process is never-ending and is meant to imbue the entire person, with the result that, in their way of thinking and acting, consecrated persons show that they belong fully and joyful to Christ; it thus demands a constant conversion to God. It aims at shaping the heart, the mind and all of life by facilitating an integration of the human, cultural, spiritual and pastoral dimensions.[33]

In a particular way, the formation of contemplatives is directed to a harmonious communion with God and one's Sisters within an atmosphere of silence protected by the daily life of the cloister.

14.   God the Father is the formator par excellence, but in this work of craftsmanship he employs human instruments. Men and women formators are elder brothers and sisters whose principal mission is that of disclosing "the beauty of following Christ and the value of the charism by which this is accomplished".[34]

Formation, especially continuing formation, is "an intrinsic requirement of religious consecration",[35] and is grounded in the daily life of the community. Consequently, sisters should keep in mind that the ordinary place where the process of formation takes place is the monastery itself, and that fraternal life in community, in all its expressions, should contribute to this process.

15.   In today's social, cultural and religious context, monasteries need to pay great attention to vocational and spiritual discernment, without yielding to the temptation to think in terms of numbers

---

[33] Cf. John Paul II, Post-Synodal Apostolic Exhortation *Vita Consecrata* (25 March 1996), 65: *AAS* 88 (1996), 441; *Code of Canon Law*, can. 664.

[34] *Ibid.*, 66: *AAS* 88 (1996), 442.

[35] *Ibid.*, 69: *AAS* 88 (1996), 444; cf. *Code of Canon Law*, can. 661.

and efficiency.[36] They should ensure that candidates receive personalized guidance and adequate programmes of formation, always keeping in mind that for initial formation and that following temporary profession, to the extent possible, "ample time must be reserved",[37] no less than nine years and not more than twelve.[38]

Prayer

16.   Liturgical and personal prayer are fundamental to, and necessary for, nourishing your contemplation. If "prayer is the 'core' of consecrated life",[39] it is even more so for the contemplative life. Today many persons do not know how to pray. Many simply feel no need to pray, or limit their relationship with God to a plea for help at times of difficulty when there is no one else to turn to. For others, prayer is merely praise in moments of happiness. In reciting and singing the praises of the Lord with the Liturgy of the Hours, you also pray for these persons and, like the prophets, you intercede for the salvation of all.[40] Personal prayer will help keep you united to the Lord like branches on the vine, and thus your life will bear abundant fruit (cf. *Jn* 15:1-15). But never forget that your life of prayer and contemplation must not be lived as a form of self-absorption; it must enlarge your heart to embrace all humanity, especially those who suffer.

Through intercessory prayer, you play a fundamental role in the life of the Church. You pray and intercede for our many brothers

---

[36] CONGREGATION FOR INSTITUTES OF CONSECRATED LIFE AND SOCIETIES OF APOSTOLIC LIFE, Instruction *Starting Afresh from Christ. A Renewed Commitment to Consecrated Life in the Third Millennium* (19 May 2002), 18.

[37] Cf. JOHN PAUL II, Post-Synodal Apostolic Exhortation *Vita Consecrata* (25 March 1996), 65: *AAS* 88 (1996), 441.

[38] Cf. *Code of Canon Law*, cann. 648 § 1 and 3; 675 § 2.

[39] *Conclusion of Holy Mass*, 2 February 2016: *L'Osservatore Romano*, 4 February 2016, p. 6; cf. *Code of Canon Law*, can. 673.

[40] Cf. SECOND VATICAN ECUMENICAL COUNCIL, Constitution *Sacrosanctum Concilium*, 83; *Code of Canon Law*, cann. 1173; 1174 § 1.

and sisters who are prisoners, migrants, refugees and victims of persecution. Your prayers of intercession embrace the many families experiencing difficulties, the unemployed, the poor, the sick, and those struggling with addiction, to mention just a few of the more urgent situations. You are like those who brought the paralytic to the Lord for healing (cf. *Mk* 2:2-12). Through your prayer, night and day, you bring before God the lives of so many of our brothers and sisters who for various reasons cannot come to him to experience his healing mercy, even as he patiently waits for them. By your prayers, you can heal the wounds of many.

The Virgin Mary is our supreme model in the contemplation of Christ. Her Son's face belongs uniquely to her. She is the Mother and Teacher of perfect conformation to her Son; by her example and her maternal presence she sustains you, her special children, in your daily fidelity to prayer (cf. *Acts* 1:14).[41]

17.   In the book of Exodus, we read that Moses decided the fate of his people by prayer; he ensured victory over the enemy as long as he kept his arms raised to ask for the Lord's help (cf. 17:11). It strikes me that this is a most eloquent image of the power and efficacy of your own prayer on behalf of all humanity and the Church, especially of the vulnerable and those in need. Now, as then, we can conclude that the fate of humanity is decided by the prayerful hearts and uplifted hands of contemplative women. That is why I urge you to remain faithful, in accordance with your constitutions, to liturgical and personal prayer; the latter is in fact a preparation for, and a prolongation of, the former. I urge you to "prefer nothing to the *opus Dei*",[42] lest anything obstruct, divert or interrupt your

---

[41] Cf. BENEDICT XVI, *Catechesis* (28 December 2011): *Insegnamenti* VII/2 (2011), 980-985; *Code of Canon Law*, can. 663 § 4; CONGREGATION FOR INSTITUTES OF CONSECRATED LIFE AND SOCIETIES OF APOSTOLIC LIFE, Instruction *The Service of Authority and Obedience* (11 May 2008), 31.

[42] BENEDICT, *Rule*, 43, 3.

ministry of prayer.[43] In this way, through contemplation you will become ever more fully an image of Christ[44] and your communities will become true schools of prayer.

18.   All this demands a spirituality grounded in the word of God, the power of the sacramental life, the teachings of the Church's magisterium and the writings of your founders and foundresses, a spirituality that enables you to become daughters of heaven and daughters of the earth, disciples and missionaries, according to your proper way of life. It also calls for gradual training in the life of personal and liturgical prayer, and contemplation itself, in the constant realization that these are chiefly nourished by the "scandalous beauty" of the cross.

The centrality of the word of God

19.   One of the most significant elements of monastic life in general is the centrality of the word of God for personal and community life. Saint Benedict stressed this when he asked his monks to listen willingly to sacred readings: *"lectiones sanctas libenter audire"*.[45] Over the centuries, monasticism has been the guardian of *lectio divina*. Nowadays this is commended to the entire People of God and demanded of all consecrated religious.[46] You yourselves are called to make it the nourishment of your contemplation and daily life, so that you can then share this transforming experience of God's word with priests, deacons, other consecrated persons and the laity. Look upon this sharing as a true ecclesial mission.

Prayer and contemplation are certainly the most fitting place to welcome the word of God, yet they themselves have their source

---

[43] Cf. FRANCIS OF ASSISI, *Regula non bullata*, XXIII, 31: FF 71.

[44] Cf. CLARE OF ASSISI, *Third Letter to Agnes of Bohemia*, 12-13: FF 2888.

[45] *Rule*, 4, 55.

[46] Cf. BENEDICT XVI, Post-Synodal Apostolic Exhortation *Verbum Domini* (30 September 2010), 86: *AAS* 102 (2010), 757; *Code of Canon Law*, can. 663 § 3.

in hearing that word. The entire Church, and especially communities completely devoted to contemplation, need to rediscover the centrality of the word of God, which, as my predecessor Saint John Paul II stated, is the "first source of all spirituality".[47] The word of God needs to nourish your life, your prayer, your contemplation and your daily journey, and to become the principle of communion for your communities and fraternities. For they are called to welcome that word, to meditate upon it, to contemplate it and to join in putting it into practice, communicating and sharing the fruits born of this experience. In this way, you will grow in an authentic spirituality of communion.[48] Here I urge you to "avoid the risk of an individualistic approach, and remember that God's word is given to us precisely to build communion, to unite us in the Truth along our path to God... Consequently, the sacred text must always be approached in the communion of the Church".[49]

20.   *Lectio divina*, the *prayerful reading of God's word*, is an art that helps us pass from the biblical text to life. It is an existential interpretation of sacred Scripture, whereby we can bridge the gap between spirituality and daily life, between faith and life. The process initiated by *lectio divina* is meant to guide us from hearing to knowledge, and from knowledge to love.

Today, thanks to the biblical renewal that received fresh impetus especially in the wake of the Dogmatic Constitution *Dei Verbum* of the Second Vatican Council, everyone is invited to familiarity with the Scriptures. Through prayerful and assiduous reading

---

[47]   JOHN PAUL II, Post-Synodal Apostolic Exhortation *Vita Consecrata* (25 March 1996), 94: *AAS* 88 (1996), 469; cf. *Code of Canon Law*, can. 758.

[48]   Cf. CONGREGATION FOR INSTITUTES OF CONSECRATED LIFE AND SOCIETIES OF APOSTOLIC LIFE Instruction *Starting Afresh From Christ: A Renewed Commitment to Consecrated Life in the Third Millennium* (19 May 2002), 25; JOHN PAUL II, Apostolic Letter *Novo Millennio Ineunte* (6 January 2001), 43: *AAS* 93 (2001), 297.

[49]   Cf. BENEDICT XVI, Post-Synodal Apostolic Exhortation *Verbum Domini* (30 September 2010), 86: *AAS* 102 (2010), 758; *Code of Canon Law*, cann. 754-755.

of the biblical text, dialogue with God becomes a daily reality for his People. *Lectio divina* should help you to cultivate a docile, wise and discerning heart (cf. *1 Kg* 3:9.12), capable of knowing what is of God and what, on the other hand, can lead away from him. *Lectio divina* should allow you to acquire that kind of supernatural intuition which enabled your founders and foundresses to avoid being conformed to the mentality of this world, but renewed in their own minds, "to discern what God's will is – his good, pleasing and perfect will" (*Rom* 12:2).[50]

21.   Your entire day, both personal and in community, ought to be organized around the word of God. Thus your communities and fraternities will become schools where the word is carefully listened to, put into practice and proclaimed to all those who encounter you.

Lastly, never forget that "the process of *lectio divina* is not concluded until it arrives at action (*actio*), which moves the believer to make his or her life a gift for others in charity"[51]. In this way, it will produce abundant fruits along the path of conformation to Christ, the goal of our entire life.

The sacraments of the Eucharist and Reconciliation

22.   The Eucharist is the sacrament par excellence of encounter with the person of Jesus; it "contains the entire spiritual wealth of the Church, that is, Christ himself".[52] The Eucharist is the heart of the life of every baptized person and of consecrated life itself; hence it is at the very core of the contemplative life. Indeed, the offering of your lives gives you a particular share in the paschal

[50] John Paul II, Post-Synodal Apostolic Exhortation *Vita Consecrata* (25 March 1996), 94: *AAS* 88 (1996), 470.

[51] Benedict XVI, Post-Synodal Apostolic Exhortation *Verbum Domini* (30 September 2010), 87: *AAS* 102 (2010), 759.

[52] Second Vatican Ecumenical Council, Decree *Presbyterorum Ordinis*, 5; cf. *Code of Canon Law*, can. 899.

mystery of death and resurrection present in the Eucharist. Our common breaking of the bread repeats and makes present Jesus' own offering of himself: the Lord "broke himself, breaks himself, for our sake" and asks us "to give ourselves, to break ourselves for the sake of others".[53] So that this profound mystery can take place and shine forth in all its richness, each celebration of the Eucharist should be prepared with care, dignity and sobriety, and all should take part in it fully, faithfully and consciously.

In the Eucharist, the eyes of the heart recognize Jesus.[54] Saint John Paul II tells us that "to contemplate Christ involves being able to recognize him wherever he manifests himself, in his many forms of presence, but above all in the living sacrament of his body and his blood. The Church draws her life from Christ in the Eucharist; she is fed by him and by him she is enlightened. The Eucharist is both a mystery of faith and a 'mystery of light'. Whenever the Church celebrates the Eucharist, the faithful can in some way relive the experience of the two disciples on the way to Emmaus: 'Their eyes were opened and they recognized him' (*Lk* 24:31)".[55] The Eucharist draws you daily into the mystery of love, nuptial love, "the redemptive act of Christ the Bridegroom towards the Church the Bride".[56]

Consequently, the tradition of prolonging the celebration of Mass with eucharistic adoration is praiseworthy; it is a privileged moment to digest spiritually the bread of the word broken during the celebration, and to persevere in thanksgiving.

---

[53] *Homily*, Solemnity of the Most Holy Body and Blood of Christ (26 May 2016): *L'Osservatore Romano*, May 27-28, 2016, p. 8; cf. *Code of Canon Law*, can. 663 § 2.

[54] Cf. JOHN PAUL II, *Homily*, Solemnity of the Most Holy Body and Blood of Christ (14 June 2001), 3: *AAS* 93 (2001), 656.

[55] ID., Encyclical Letter *Ecclesia de Eucharistia* (17 April 2003), 6: *AAS* 95 (2003), 437.

[56] ID., Apostolic Letter *Mulieris Dignitatem* (15 August 1988), 26: *AAS* 80 (1988), 1716.

23.   The Eucharist inspires a commitment to continuous conversion that finds sacramental expression in Reconciliation. May frequent personal or communal celebration of the sacrament of Penance become a privileged means for you to contemplate Jesus Christ, the face of the Father's mercy,[57] to be renewed in heart and to purify your relationship with God in contemplation.

The joyful experience of God's forgiveness received in this sacrament grants you the grace to become prophets and ministers of his mercy, and instruments of reconciliation, forgiveness and peace. Our world greatly needs such prophets and ministers.

Fraternal life in community

24.   Fraternal life in community is an essential element of religious life in general, and of monastic life in particular, albeit in the variety of different charisms.

The relationship of communion is the manifestation of that love which wells up in the heart of the Father and is poured into our hearts by the Spirit whom Jesus has bestowed on us. Simply by making this reality visible, the Church, God's family, is the sign of profound union with him and appears as the home in which this life-giving experience is possible for all. By calling men and women to share in his life, Christ the Lord formed a community that makes visible "the capacity for the communion of goods, for fraternal love, for shared projects and activities; and this capacity comes from having accepted the invitation to follow him more freely and more closely".[58] The fraternal life, in virtue of which consecrated men and women seek to become "one heart and one soul" (*Acts* 4:32)

---

[57] Cf. Bull *Misericordiae Vultus*, 1: *AAS* 107 (2015), 399; cf. *Code of Canon Law*, cann. 664; 630.

[58] CONGREGATION FOR INSTITUTES OF CONSECRATED LIFE AND SOCIETIES OF APOSTOLIC LIFE, Instruction *Fraternal Life in Community. "Congregavit nos in unum Christi amor"* (2 February 1994), 10.

on the model of the earliest Christian communities, "aims to be an eloquent witness to the Trinity".[59]

25. Fraternal communion is a reflection of God's own way of being and bestowing himself; it testifies to the fact that "God is love" (*1 Jn* 4:8, 16). The consecrated life professes to believe in, and live by, the love of the Father, the Son and the Holy Spirit. The community of brothers and sisters thus becomes a graced reflection of the God who is a Trinity of Love.

Unlike the life of hermits, who live "in silence and solitude"[60] and are likewise esteemed by the Church, the monastic life entails a growing community life meant to create an authentic fraternal communion, a *koinonia*. This means that all the members must see themselves as builders of community and not simply recipients of its eventual benefits. A community exists inasmuch as it comes about and is built up by the contribution of all, each according to his or her gifts, through the development of a strong spirituality of communion whereby all experience a sense of belonging.[61] Only in this way can life in community provide its members with the mutual assistance needed to live their vocation to the full.[62]

26. You who have embraced the monastic life must never forget that today's men and women expect you to bear witness to an authentic fraternal communion that, in a society marked by divisions and inequality, clearly demonstrates that life in common is both possible and fulfilling (cf. *Ps* 133:1), despite differences of age, education and even culture. Your communities ought to be credible

---

[59] JOHN PAUL II, Post-Synodal Apostolic Exhortation *Vita Consecrata* (25 March 1996), 21: *AAS* 88 (1996), 395.

[60] *Code of Canon Law*, can. 603.

[61] Cf. JOHN PAUL II, Apostolic Letter *Novo Millennio Ineunte* (6 January 2001), 43: *AAS* 93 (2001), 296-297.

[62] Cf. SECOND VATICAN ECUMENICAL COUNCIL, Decree *Perfectae Caritatis*, 15; *Code of Canon Law*, can. 602.

signs that these differences, far from being an obstacle to fraternal life, actually enrich it. Remember that unity and communion are not the same as uniformity, and are nourished by dialogue, sharing, mutual assistance and profound compassion, especially towards the most frail and needy.

27.   Lastly, remember that fraternal life in community is also the primary form of evangelization: "By this everyone will know that you are my disciples, if you love one another" (*Jn* 13:34-35). For this reason, I urge you not to neglect the means suggested and provided by the Church to consolidate community life[63] and to be ever vigilant with regard to this sensitive but fundamental aspect of monastic life. Together with sharing the word and the experience of God, and communal discernment, "we should recall fraternal correction, review of life and other forms typical of the tradition. These are concrete ways of putting at the service of others and of pouring into the community the gifts which the Spirit gives so abundantly for its upbuilding and for its mission in the world".[64]

As I urged during my recent meeting with consecrated persons in Rome for the conclusion of the Year of Consecrated Life,[65] try to remain close to your sisters, whom the Lord has given you as a precious gift. Then too, as Saint Benedict reminds us, in community life it is essential both to "honour the elderly and to show affection to the young".[66] The fruitfulness of fraternal life in community is also rooted in this effort to reconcile the remembrance of the past with the promise of the future.

---

[63] Cf. CONGREGATION FOR INSTITUTES OF CONSECRATED LIFE AND SOCIETIES OF APOSTOLIC LIFE, Instruction *Fraternal Life in Community. "Congregavit nos in unum Christi amor"* (2 February 1994); *Code of Canon Law,* cann. 607 § 2; 608; 665; 699 § 1.

[64] *Ibid.*, 32; cf. *Code of Canon Law,* cann. 619; 630; 664.

[65] Cf. *Address to Participants in the Jubilee of Consecrated Life*, 1 February 2016: *L'Osservatore Romano,* 1-2 February 2016, p. 8.

[66] BENEDICT, *Rule*, IV, 70-71.

The autonomy of monasteries

28.   Autonomy favours the stability of life and internal unity of each community, ensuring the best conditions for contemplation. But autonomy ought not to mean independence or isolation, especially from the other monasteries of the same Order or the same charismatic family.

29.   "No one contributes to the future in isolation, by his or her efforts alone, but by seeing himself or herself as part of a true communion which is constantly open to encounter, dialogue, attentive listening and mutual assistance".[67]   For this reason, take care to avoid "the disease of self-absorption"[68] and to preserve the value of communion between different monasteries as a path of openness towards the future and a means of updating and giving expression to the enduring and codified values of your autonomy.[69]

Federations

30.   Federation is an important structure of communion between monasteries sharing the same charism, lest they remain isolated.

The principal aim of a Federation is to promote the contemplative life in the member monasteries, in accordance with the demands of their proper charism, and to ensure assistance in initial and continuous formation as well as in practical needs, through the exchange of nuns and the sharing of material goods.   In view of these aims, federations ought to be encouraged and increase in number.[70]

---

[67] *Apostolic Letter to All Consecrated Persons for the Year of Consecrated Life* (21 November 2014), II, 3: *AAS* 106 (2014), 943.

[68] *Ibid.*

[69] Cf. *ibid.*; *Code of Canon Law,* cann. 614-615; 628 § 2-1; 630 § 3; 638 § 4; 684 § 3; 688 § 2; 699 § 2; 708; 1428 § 1-2.

[70] Cf. *Code of Canon Law,* cann. 582; 684 § 3.

The cloister

31.   Separation from the world, necessary for all those who follow
Christ in the religious life, is especially evident in your own case, as
contemplative sisters, by the cloister, which is the inner sanctum of
the Church as spouse: "a sign of the exclusive union of the Church
as Bride with her Lord, whom she loves above all things".[71]

The cloister has taken canonical shape in four diverse forms
and degrees.[72] In addition to that common to all religious institutes, there are three others typical of contemplative communities, namely papal, constitutional and monastic. The papal cloister "conforms to the norms given by the Apostolic See"[73] and
"excludes any external ministry".[74] The constitutional cloister is
defined by the rules of individual constitutions, while the monastic
cloister, though maintaining the character of "a more rigorous discipline"[75] with respect to the common cloister, may, in addition to
their primary function of divine worship, allow for a wider range
of hospitality and reception, always in accordance with the individual constitutions. The common cloister is the least restrictive
of the four.[76]

The variety of ways in which the cloister is observed within
the same Order should be seen as an enrichment and not an obstacle to communion; it is a matter of reconciling different approaches
in a higher unity.[77] This communion can take concrete shape in

[71] JOHN PAUL II, Post-Synodal Apostolic Exhortation *Vita Consecrata*
(25 March 1996), 59: *AAS* 88 (1996), 431.
   [72] Cf. *ibid.*, 59; *Code of Canon Law,* can. 667.
   [73] *Code of Canon Law,* can. 667 § 3.
   [74] *Ibid.*, can. 674.
   [75] *Ibid.*, can. 667 § 2.
   [76] Cf. *ibid.*, can. 667 § 1.
   [77] Cf. J. M. BERGOGLIO, *Intervention* (13 October 1994) at the Synod of Bishops on
Consecrated Life and its Mission in the Church and in the World (in *"Vida Religiosa"*,
115/7: July-September 2013).

various forms of encounter and cooperation, above all in initial and ongoing formation.[78]

Work

32.   Through your labour too, you share in the work that God the Creator carries out in the world. This activity puts you in close relationship with all those who labour responsibly to live by the fruit of their toil (cf. *Gen* 3:19) and thus to contribute to the work of creation and the service of humanity. In a particular way, it shows your solidarity with the poor who cannot live without work, and who, even though they may work, still frequently need the providential help of their brothers and sisters.

As the great contemplative saints have warned, work must never stifle the spirit of contemplation. Your life is meant to be "poor in fact and spent in hardworking moderation" – as your solemnly professed vow of evangelical poverty requires.[79] For this reason, your work should be done carefully and faithfully, without yielding to the present-day culture and its mindset of efficiency and constant activity. The *"ora et labora"* of the Benedictine tradition should always be your inspiration and help you to find the right balance between seeking the Absolute and commitment to your daily chores, between the peace of contemplation and the effort expended in work.

Silence

33.   In the contemplative life, and especially in the wholly contemplative life, I consider it important to heed the silence filled by God's presence as the necessary "space" for hearing and pondering his word (*ruminatio*). Silence is a prerequisite to that gaze of faith

---

[78] Cf. Apostolic Letter to All Consecrated Persons for the Year of Consecrated Life (21 November 2014), II, 3: *AAS* 106 (2014), 942-943.
[79] Cf. *Code of Canon Law,* can. 600.

which enables us to welcome God's presence into our own life, that of the brothers and sisters given us by the Lord, and the events of today's world. Silence entails self-emptying in order to grow in receptivity; interior noise makes it impossible to welcome anyone or anything. Your wholly contemplative life calls for "time and the ability to be silent and listen"[80] to God and the plea of humanity. Moved by the love each one of you has for the Lord, let your bodily tongue fall silent and allow that of the Spirit to speak.[81]

In this, Mary Most Holy can serve as your example. She was able to receive the Word because she was a woman of silence – no barren or empty silence, but rather one rich and overflowing. The silence of the Virgin Mother was also full of love, for love always prepares us to welcome the Other and others.

The communications media

34.   In our society, the digital culture has a decisive influence in shaping our thoughts and the way we relate to the world and, in particular, to other people. Contemplative communities are not immune from this cultural climate. Clearly, these media can prove helpful for formation and communication. At the same time, I urge a prudent discernment aimed at ensuring that they remain truly at the service of formation to contemplative life and necessary communication, and do not become occasions for wasting time or escaping from the demands of fraternal life in community. Nor should they prove harmful for your vocation or become an obstacle to your life wholly dedicated to contemplation.[82]

---

[80] *Message for the 48ᵗʰ World Communications Day* (1 June 2014): *AAS* 106 (2014), 114; cf. Congregation for Institutes of Consecrated Life and Societies of Apostolic Life, Instruction *Fraternal Life in Community. "Congregavit nos in unum Christi amor"* (2 February 1994), 10 and 34.

[81] Cf. Clare of Assisi, *Fourth Letter to Agnes*, 35: FF 2908.

[82] Cf. *Code of Canon Law*, can. 666.

35.   The practice of asceticism, by drawing upon all those means that the Church proposes for self-control and the purification of the heart, is also a path to liberation from "worldliness". Asceticism fosters a life in accordance with the interior logic of the Gospel, which is that of gift, especially the gift of self as the natural response to the first and only love of your life. In this way, you will be able to respond not only to the expectations of your brothers and sisters, but also to the moral and spiritual demands inherent in the three evangelical counsels that you professed with a solemn vow.[83]

Your life of complete self-giving thus takes on a powerful prophetic meaning. Your moderation, your detachment from material things, your self-surrender in obedience, your transparent relationships – these become all the more radical and demanding as a result of your free renunciation "of 'space', of contacts, of so many benefits of creation... [as a] particular way of offering up [your] 'body'".[84] Your choice of a life of stability becomes an eloquent sign of fidelity for our globalized world, accustomed to increasingly rapid and easy relocation, with the risk that many persons never sink roots in any one place.

In the life of the cloister, fraternal relationships become even more demanding,[85] since interaction in such communities is constant and close. By remaining close to your brothers and sisters despite disagreements needing to be settled, tensions and conflicts to be resolved, and weaknesses to be accepted, you set a helpful example to the People of God and to today's world, so often rent

---

[83] Cf. *Conclusion of Holy Mass*, 2 February 2016: *L'Osservatore Romano*, February 4, 2016, p. 6; *Code of Canon Law*, cann. 599-601; 1191-1192.

[84] JOHN PAUL II, Post-Synodal Apostolic Exhortation *Vita Consecrata* (25 March 1996), 59: *AAS* 88 (1996), 431.

[85] CONGREGATION FOR INSTITUTES OF CONSECRATED LIFE AND SOCIETIES OF APOSTOLIC LIFE, Instruction *Fraternal Life in Community. "Congregavit nos in unum Christi amor"* (2 February 1994), 10.

by conflict and division. The path of asceticism is also a means of acknowledging your own weakness and entrusting it to the tender mercy of God and the community.

Finally, the commitment to asceticism is necessary for carrying out with love and fidelity our daily responsibilities, for seeing them as opportunities to share in the lot of our many brothers and sisters throughout the world, and as a silent and fruitful offering for their needs.

THE WITNESS OFFERED BY NUNS

36.   Dear sisters, everything that I have written in this Apostolic Constitution is meant to be, for you who have embraced the contemplative vocation, an effective contribution to the renewal of your life and your mission in the Church and the world. May the Lord be ever present and active in your heart and transform you entirely in him, the ultimate aim of the contemplative life,[86] and may your communities or fraternities become true schools of contemplation and prayer.

The world and the Church need you to be beacons of light for the journey of the men and women of our time. This should be your prophetic witness. You have chosen not to flee the world out of fear, as some might think, but to remain in the world, while not being of the world (cf. *Jn* 18:19). Although you live apart from the world, through the signs of your belonging to Christ, you tirelessly intercede for mankind, presenting to the Lord its fears and hopes, its joys and sufferings.[87]

Do not deprive us of your participation in building an ever more humane and thus evangelical world. In union with the Lord, hear

---

[86] Cf. CLARE OF ASSISI, *Third Letter to Agnes*, 12-13: FF 2888; *Fourth Letter to Agnes*, 15-16: FF 2902.

[87] Cf. SECOND VATICAN ECUMENICAL COUNCIL, Pastoral Constitution *Gaudium et Spes*, 4.

the cry of your brothers and sisters (cf. *Ex* 3:7; *Jas* 5:4) who are victims of the "throwaway culture",[88] or simply in need of the light brought by the Gospel. Practice the art of listening "which is more than simply hearing",[89] and the "spirituality of hospitality", by taking to heart and bringing to prayer all that concerns our brothers and sisters made in the image and likeness of God (cf. *Gen* 1:26). As I noted in the Apostolic Exhortation *Evangelii Gaudium*, "intercessory prayer does not divert us from true contemplation, since authentic contemplation always has a place for others".[90]

In this way, your testimony will be, as it were, a necessary complement to the witness of those who, as contemplatives in the heart of the world, bear witness to the Gospel while remaining fully immersed in the work of building the earthly city.

37.   Dear contemplative sisters, you are well aware that your form of consecrated life, like all other forms, "is a gift to the Church, arises and grows within the Church, and is completely directed to the good of the Church".[91] Persevere, then, in profound communion with the Church so that in her midst you may become a living continuation of the mystery of Mary, Virgin, Bride and Mother, who welcomes and treasures the Word in order to give it back to the world. Thus you will help to bring Christ to birth and increase in the hearts of men and women who, often unconsciously, are thirsting for the One who is the "way, the truth, and the life (*Jn* 14:6). Like Mary, you too strive to be a "stairway" by which God descends to encounter humanity, and humanity ascends to encounter God and to contemplate his face in the face of Christ.

---

[88] Apostolic Exhortation *Evangelii Gaudium* (24 Novembre 2013), 53: *AAS* 105 (2013), 1042; cf. ibid., 187ff: *AAS* 105 (2013), 1098ff.

[89] *Ibid.*, 171: *AAS* 105 (2013), 1091.

[90] *Ibid.*, 281: *AAS* 105 (2013), 1133.

[91] Cf. J. M. BERGOGLIO, *Intervention* (13 October 1994) at the Synod of Bishops on *Consecrated Life and its Mission in the Church and in the World* (in *"Vida Religiosa"* 115/7, July-September 2013).

CONCLUSION AND REGULATIONS

In the light of the above, I decree and establish the following.

Art. 1. With reference to canon 20 of the *Code of Canon Law*, and after a careful study of the above 37 articles, with the promulgation and the publication of this Apostolic Constitution *Vultum Dei Quaerere,* the following are derogated:

1. Those canons of the *Code of Canon Law* that, in part, directly contradict any article of the present Constitution;
2. and, more specifically, the articles containing norms and dispositions found in:
   - the Apostolic Constitution *Sponsa Christi* of Pius XII (21 November 1950): *Statuta Generalia Monialium*;
   - the Instruction *Inter Praeclara* of the Sacred Congregation for Religious (23 November 1950);
   - the Instruction *Verbi Sponsa* of the Congregation for Institutes of Consecrated Life and Societies of Apostolic Life (13 May 1999) on the contemplative life and enclosure of nuns.

Art. 2 §1. This Constitution is addressed to the Congregation for Institutes of Consecrated Life and Societies of Apostolic Life, and to individual cloistered monasteries of nuns, whether wholly contemplative or not, and whether part of a federation or not.

§2. The matters regulated by this Apostolic Constitution are those listed above in No. 12 and further developed in Nos. 13-35.

§3. The Congregation for Institutes of Consecrated Life and Societies of Apostolic Life – if need be, in agreement with the Congregation for the Oriental Churches and the Congregation for the Evangelization of Peoples – will regulate the different modalities of implementing these constitutive norms, in accordance with the different monastic traditions and taking into account the various charismatic families.

Art. 3 §1. Through suitable structures identified during the elaboration of a plan of community life, individual monasteries are to give special attention to ongoing formation, which is the foundation for every stage of formation, beginning with initial formation.

§2. In order to ensure adequate ongoing formation, federations are to promote cooperation between monasteries through the exchange of formational materials and the use of digital means of communication, always exercising due discretion.

§3. Together with the careful selection of sisters to serve as formators and to guide candidates in the development of personal maturity, individual monasteries and federations are to make every effort to ensure a sound preparation of formators and their assistants.

§4. Sisters charged with the sensitive task of formation may also attend, *servatis de iure servandis*, specific courses on formation outside their monastery, always conducting themselves in a way fitting and consistent with their own charism. The Congregation for Institutes of Consecrated Life and Societies of Apostolic Life is to issue particular norms in this regard.

§5. Monasteries are to pay special attention to vocational and spiritual discernment, ensuring that candidates receive personalized guidance, and to provide adequate programmes of formation, always keeping in mind that ample time is to be set apart for initial formation.

§6. Even though the establishment of international and multicultural communities is a sign of the universality of the charism, the recruitment of candidates from other countries solely for the sake of ensuring the survival of a monastery is to be absolutely avoided. To ensure that this is the case, certain criteria are to be determined.

§7. To ensure a high quality of formation, monasteries should, as circumstances dictate, promote common houses for initial formation.

Art. 4 § 1. Recognizing that prayer is the heart of contemplative life, each monastery is to review its daily horarium to see if it is centred on the Lord.

§ 2. Community celebrations should be reviewed to see if they constitute an authentic and vital encounter with the Lord.

Art. 5 § 1. Given the importance of *lectio divina*, each monastery is to establish fitting times and means for respecting this requirement of reading and listening, *ruminatio*, prayer, contemplation and sharing of the sacred Scriptures.

§ 2. Since sharing the transforming experience of God's word with priests, deacons, other consecrated persons and the laity is an expression of genuine ecclesial communion, each monastery is to determine how this spiritual outreach can be accomplished.

Art. 6 § 1. Each monastery, in elaborating its plan of community and fraternal life, in addition to carefully preparing its eucharistic celebrations, is to set aside appropriate times for eucharistic adoration, also inviting the faithful of the local Church to take part.

§ 2. Particular attention is to be given to the selection of chaplains, confessors and spiritual directors, taking into account the specific charism and the demands of fraternal life in community.

Art. 7 § 1. Those called to carry out the ministry of authority, besides being attentive to their own formation, are to be guided by a true spirit of fraternity and service so as to foster a joy-filled environment of freedom and responsibility, thus promoting personal and community discernment and truthful communication of what each member does, thinks and feels.

§ 2. The plan of community life should readily welcome and encourage the sharing of each sister's human and spiritual gifts for mutual enrichment and growth in fraternity.

Art. 8 § 1. Juridical autonomy needs to be matched by a genuine autonomy of life. This entails a certain, even minimal, number of sisters, provided that the majority are not elderly, the vitality needed to practice and spread the charism, a real capacity to provide for formation and governance, dignity and quality of liturgical, fraternal and spiritual life, sign value and participation in life of the local Church, self-sufficiency and a suitably appointed monastery building. These criteria ought to be considered comprehensively and in an overall perspective.

§2. Whenever the requirements for a monastery's genuine autonomy are lacking, the Congregation for Institutes of Consecrated Life and Societies of Apostolic Life will study the possibility of establishing an *ad hoc* commission made up of the ordinary, the president of the federation, a representative of the federation and the abbess or prioress of the monastery. In every case, the purpose of this intervention is to initiate a process of guidance for the revitalization of the monastery, or to effect its closure.

§3. This process may also envisage affiliation to another monastery or entrustment, if the monastery belongs to a federation, to the federation president and her council. In every case, the ultimate decision always rests with the Congregation for Institutes of Consecrated Life and Societies of Apostolic Life.

Art. 9 §1. Initially, all monasteries are to be part of a federation. If, for some special reason, a monastery cannot join a federation, after the vote of the chapter, permission to allow the monastery to remain outside a federation is to be sought from the Holy See, which is competent to study and decide the question.

§2. Federations can be established not only on a geographical basis but also on an affinity of spirit and traditions. Norms in this regard will be issued by the Congregation for Institutes of Consecrated Life and Societies of Apostolic Life.

§3. Assistance in formation and in meeting concrete needs through the exchange of nuns and the sharing of material goods is also to be ensured, in accordance with the provisions of the

Congregation for Institutes of Consecrated Life and Societies of Apostolic Life. The Congregation will also determine the competencies of the federation president and council.

§4. The association, even juridical, of monasteries to the corresponding Order of men is to be encouraged. Confederations and the establishment of international commissions made up of different Orders, with statutes approved by the Congregation for Institutes of Consecrated Life and Societies of Apostolic Life, are likewise to be encouraged.

Art. 10 §1. Each monastery, following serious discernment and respecting its proper tradition and the demands of its constitutions, is to ask the Holy See what form of cloister it wishes to embrace, whenever a different form of cloister from the present one is called for.

§2. Once one of the possible forms of cloister is chosen and approved, each monastery will take care to comply with, and live in accordance with, its demands.

Art. 11 §1. Even if certain monastic communities, in accordance with their proper law, may enjoy some income, this does not mean that the members are exempted from the obligation of labour.

§2. In communities devoted to contemplation, the income received from labour should not be used exclusively to ensure a decent sustenance, but also, if possible, to assist the poor and monasteries in need.

Art. 12. The daily horarium is to include suitable moments of silence, in order to foster a climate of prayer and contemplation.

Art. 13. In its plan of community life, each monastery is to provide for some fitting means for expressing the ascetic discipline of monastic life, in order to make it more prophetic and credible.

Final Provision

Art. 14 §1. The Congregation for Institutes of Consecrated Life and Societies of Apostolic Life will issue, in accordance with the spirit and the norms of the present Apostolic Constitution, a new Instruction concerning the matters dealt with in No. 12.

§2. Once they have been adapted to the new regulations, the articles of the constitutions or rules of individual institutes are to be submitted for approval by the Holy See.

Given in Rome, at Saint Peter's, on 29 June, the Solemnity of Saints Peter and Paul, in the year 2016, the fourth of my Pontificate.

Franciscus

VATICAN PRESS

Made in the USA
Monee, IL
28 August 2021